Quiet Moments and a Cup of Tea

CHARMING STORIES TO GRACE YOUR DAY

Compiled by **ALICE GRAY**

Artwork by **SUSAN MINK COLCLOUGH**

Blue Cottage Gifts™, a division of
Multnomah Publishers, Inc.®
Sisters, OR 97759

QUIET MOMENTS AND A CUP OF TEA
©2001 by Blue Cottage Gifts™
Published by Blue Cottage Gifts™, a division of
Multnomah Publishers, Inc.®
P.O. Box 1720, Sisters, OR 97759

ISBN 1-58860-008-4

Artwork by Susan Mink Colclough
Artwork designs by Susan are reproduced under license from ©Arts Uniq', Inc.®,
Cookeville, TN and may not be reproduced without permission. For information
regarding art prints featured in this book, please contact:
Arts Uniq', Inc.
P.O. Box 3085
Cookeville, TN 38502
1-800-223-5020

Designed by Koechel Peterson & Associates, Minneapolis, Minnesota

Please see the acknowledgments at the back of the book for complete attributions for
this material.

Printed in China

01 02 03 04 05 06—10 9 8 7 6 5 4 3 2 1 0

www.gift-talk.com

Contents

Quiet Moments and a Cup of Tea

"Where there's tea," wrote a wise sage, "there's hope."

I have to agree. A cup of hot tea—whether served in elegant bone china, or sipped from a plain, well-loved cup on a languid afternoon by the sea—represents those scarce, quiet corners in our lives. And how we need such moments! People speak of "a quick cup of coffee," but tea—ah, tea must be savored…just as time alone is savored.

Peaceful moments are the rarest of treasures. We would love to extend those intervals of rest, reflection, and repose. When I am alone with my thoughts, a steaming cup of tea soothes my spirit and provides a canopy of serenity where I can reflect on the beauty and blessings of life.

Great-grandma Jewel, a delightful lady who lived to the age of 108, told her friends that "tea is a cup of life." I know just what she means. So many memories visit those wistful moments…and hope, like fine, white sugar, sweetens the hour with promise.

So nestle into your quiet corner, my friend. Breathe a long, contented sigh, and treasure the warm cup you hold in your hand. May the stories within these lovely pages refresh your spirit and bring tranquility to your busy day.

The Guest Book

CARLA MUIR

When I was young, I'd visit folks
who lived on neighboring streets.
A widow often asked me in
for tea and pastry treats.

She made me feel special with
a table set just so,
while she would talk of baking and
how long to raise the dough.

Politely, I would listen although
thoughts would often stray.
Each time I left, I gave my word
I'd come another day.

Before I went to college
she asked that I stop by.
She opened up her old guest book
while trying not to cry.

Then as she paged through many years,
in pen I saw my name.
For she had written in that book
the days and times I came.

"You won't learn this in textbooks,"
she softly said to me—
"how you can lift another's soul
with just a cup of tea."

That Little China Chip

BETTIE B. YOUNGS

One day when I was about nine years old, my mother took a trip into town and put me in charge of my brothers and sisters. As she drove away, I ran into her bedroom and opened the dresser to snoop.

There in the top drawer, beneath soft, wonderful-smelling grown-up garments, was a small wooden jewelry box. I was fascinated by its treasures—the ruby ring left to my mother by her favorite aunt; pearl earrings that once belonged to my grandmother; my mother's own wedding band, which she took off to do farm chores alongside my father.

I tried them all on, filling my mind with glorious images of what it must be like to be a beautiful woman like my mother and to own such exquisite things.

Then I saw there was something tucked behind the piece of red felt lining the lid. Lifting the cloth, I found a little white chip of china.

I picked it up. Why in the world did my mother keep this broken thing? Glinting slightly in the light, it offered no answers.

Some months later, I was setting the dinner table when our neighbor Marge knocked at the door. Mom, busy at the stove, called to her to come in. Glancing at the table, Marge said, "Oh, you're expecting company. I'll stop by another time."

"No, come on in," Mom replied. "We're not expecting anyone."

"But isn't that your good china?" Marge asked. "I'd never trust kids to handle my good dishes!"

Mom laughed. "Tonight's my family's favorite meal. If you set your best table for a special meal with special guests, why not for your family?"

"But your beautiful china!" responded Marge.

"Oh, well," said Mom, "a few broken plates are a small price to pay for the joy we get using them." Then she added, "Besides, every chip and crack has a story to tell."

Reaching into the cupboard, Mom pulled out an old, pieced-together plate. "This one shattered the day we brought Mark home from the hospital," she said. "What a cold and blustery afternoon that was! Judy was only six, but she wanted to be helpful. She dropped the plate carrying it to the sink.

"At first I was upset, but then I told myself, 'I

won't let a broken plate change the happiness we feel welcoming our new baby.' Besides, we all had a lot of fun gluing it together!"

Marge looked doubtful.

Mom went to the cupboard again and took down another plate. Holding it up, she said, "See this break on the edge here? It happened when I was seventeen."

Her voice softened. "One fall day my brothers needed help putting up the last of the fall hay, so they hired a young man to help out. He was slim, with powerful arms and thick blond hair. He had an incredible smile.

"My brothers took a liking to him and invited him to dinner. When my older brother sat the young man next to me, it flustered me so, I nearly fainted."

Suddenly remembering that she was telling the story to her young daughter and a neighbor, Mom blushed and hurried on. "Well, he handed me his plate and asked for a helping. But I was so nervous that when I took the plate, it slipped and knocked against the casserole dish."

"That sounds like a memory I'd try to forget," said Marge.

"Oh, no," countered my mother. "As the young man was leaving, he walked over, took my hand in his, and laid a piece of broken china in my palm. He didn't

say a word. He just smiled that smile.

"One year later I married him. And to this day, when I see this plate, I fondly recall the moment I met him."

Seeing me staring, Mom gave me a wink. Then, carefully, she put the plate back, behind the others, in a place all its own.

I couldn't forget about that plate with the missing chip. At the first chance, I went up to Mom's room and took out the little wooden jewelry box again. There was the small shard of china.

I examined it carefully, then I ran to the kitchen cupboard, pulled over a chair, climbed up and took down a plate. Just as I had guessed, the chip my mother had so carefully saved belonged to the plate she broke on the day she met my father.

Wiser now, and with more respect, I cautiously returned the chip to its place among the jewels.

The love story that began with that chip is now in its fifty-fourth year. Recently one of my sisters asked Mom if someday the antique ruby ring could be hers. My other sister has laid claim to Grandmother's pearl earrings.

As for me, I'd like Mom's most precious keepsake, a memento of an extraordinary life of loving; that little china chip.

She was a fine woman, a perfect gentlewoman. She had taken life, as she liked a cup of tea — weak, with an exquisite aroma and plenty of cream and sugar.

HENRY JAMES

A Mailbox Mercy

NANCY JO SULLIVAN
from Moments of Grace

It was late afternoon, Valentine's Day. I was mad at my mom. Though it had been weeks since the argument, a silly argument, I still found myself brooding.

"Why should I be the one to apologize?" I told myself as I signed my name to a valentine I had bought out of obligation.

"No 'I love yous' from me," I said as I smacked a stamp on the red envelope.

Moments later, I drove to the post office. Amid the pink shadows of a February sunset, I steered my van into a line of cars waiting at the drop-in mailbox.

Minutes passed. The post office traffic remained at a standstill. Rolling down my van window, I noticed a rusted station wagon at the front of the car line.

Was the car stalled at the mailbox?

Soon, a well-dressed woman in a red Cavalier became impatient with the wait. She honked at the station wagon, loudly, holding her horn down in anger.

Startled by the horn, an elderly man hobbled from the rusted sedan. Holding a cane to balance his uneven gait, he shuffled to the mailbox, clutching a stack of red-enveloped valentines.

"I'm sorry," he called out to the woman, his voice soft and trembling.

In an instant, the woman opened her car door and rushed to the old man's side, throwing her arms around his shoulders.

"I'm sorry," I heard her say.

In the last sunlit rays of the day, the man gently patted her on the back, resting one hand on his cane.

As I watched from my windshield, I realized that these two strangers had given me a fresh perspective on a passage I had long since committed to memory: "If you forgive others, your heavenly Father will forgive you."

Suddenly, I realized that I had been wasting my time, harboring unforgiveness in my heart, waiting for my mother's apology.

While honking the "horn" of anger, I had placed all the blame for the argument on my mom, refusing to acknowledge the hurtful words I had spoken to her.

I needed to ask for her forgiveness.

I also needed to offer her the same kind of mercy I had just witnessed at the mailbox—the unconditional mercy of God.

As the old man and the well-dressed woman parted, the line of cars began to move in a steady pace towards the mailbox.

With one hand on the steering wheel, I carefully reopened my mother's card.

Now one car away from the drop box, I quickly rewrote a new Valentine's greeting:

"I'm sorry—I love you, Mom."

Practice tenderhearted mercy and kindness to others...be gentle and ready to forgive; never hold grudges... most of all, let love guide your life.

COLOSSIANS 3:12-13, TLB

Picture of Peace

CATHERINE MARSHALL

There once was a king who offered a prize to the artist who would paint the best picture of peace. Many artists tried. The king looked at all the pictures. But there were only two he really liked, and he had to choose between them.

One picture was of a calm lake. The lake was a perfect mirror for peaceful towering mountains all around it. Overhead was a blue sky with fluffy white clouds. All who saw this picture thought that it was a perfect picture of peace.

The other picture had mountains, too. But these were rugged and bare. Above was an angry sky, from which rain fell and in which lightning played. Down the side of the mountain tumbled a foaming waterfall. This did not look peaceful at all.

But when the king looked closely, he saw behind the waterfall a tiny bush growing in a crack in the rock. In the bush a mother bird had built her nest. There, in the midst of the rush of angry water, sat the mother bird on her nest—in perfect peace.

Which picture do you think won the prize? The king chose the second picture. Do you know why?

"Because," explained the king, "peace does not mean to be in a place where there is no noise, trouble, or hard work. Peace means to be in the midst of all those things and still be calm in your heart. That is the real meaning of peace."

To live with serenity does not necessarily mean that outward conditions have changed. Serenity is an inner peace that is present even in difficult surroundings.

WILLIAM V. PIETSON

A Time to Scatter

MARY PIELENZ HAMPTON
from A Tea for All Seasons

One afternoon when I was about 18 years old, I left our house and walked the four blocks to the downtown area, hoping to find someone or something to lift my spirits.

I found a friend working at a shop, and her day was even worse than mine. As I walked on though, I passed an open-air flower stand with some of the season's first daffodils. Their cheerful sunniness stood out in dramatic contrast to the drippy gray of the streets and the skies. I purchased a half dozen, knowing that they would brighten my room at home.

On the way home, I stopped and gave a couple of them to my friend, hoping to cheer her up. A little bit further along my route, I encountered a lighthearted street person who commented on the flowers. I gave him one, too.

At the last corner before my house, there was a shop that I passed nearly every day on my way to and from church and school. My path often crossed with a man who worked there—his big, booming voice a disconcerting contrast to the disabled body in his wheelchair. His greeting was always warm and friendly, but I was intimidated and usually kept my response brief as I hurried on my way.

On this day, my feet took over and I walked past the crosswalk and into the store before my mind had a chance to stop them. I walked up to the counter, and thrust the three remaining daffodils toward him saying, "These are for you, because daffodils are cheerful and you're always cheerful." Still in disbelief at what I had done, I turned and left before he had an opportunity to respond.

I walked home the remaining block a different person. Even though I went without the flowers that I had purchased to cheer myself, the sunshine that came from my heart illuminated my path as though the sun itself had broken through the clouds. The simple act of giving away something that I wanted changed me. I was no longer intimidated by the man at the shop in the corner. I had seen a glimmer that I could be a giving person.

Peace does not dwell in outward things,
but within the soul. FRANÇOIS FÉNELON

The Seven Wonders

AUTHOR UNKNOWN

The teacher asked her students to make a list of the seven natural wonders of the world. The class set to work on the project for quite a while, and as time wore on some of the students finished the list. The teacher said the children could go outside for recess as each one finished. Eventually, only one little girl was still at her desk writing. Then she smiled, wrote something, and jumped up, joyfully announcing that she was done and skipped happily out to play with the others. The teacher picked up the paper and read the following:

1. Seeing   5. Running

2. Hearing   6. Laughing

3. Tasting   7. Loving

4. Touching

God's goodness hath been great to thee —
Let never day or night unhallowed pass but still
remember what the Lord hath done.

WILLIAM SHAKESPEARE

A Perfect Pot of Tea

ROBERTA MESSNER

An impatient crowd of nearly two hundred die-hard bargain hunters shoved their way into the huge living room of the old Witherses homestead. The sweltering ninety-degree temperature didn't deter a single one, all in pursuit of the estate sale find of the summer.

The lady conducting the sale, a long-time acquaintance, nodded as we watched the early morning scavengers. "How's this for bedlam?" she chuckled.

I smiled in agreement. "I shouldn't even be here. I have to be at the airport in less than an hour," I admitted to her. "But when I was a teenager, I sold cosmetics in this neighborhood. And Hillary Withers was my favorite customer."

32

"Then run and check out the attic," she suggested. "There are plenty of old cosmetics up there."

Quickly, I squeezed through the ever-growing throng and climbed the stairs to the third floor. The attic was deserted except for a petite elderly woman presiding over several tables loaded with yellowed bags of all sizes.

"What brings you all the way up here?" she asked as she popped the stopper out of a perfume bottle. "There's nothing up here except old Avon, Tupperware, and Fuller Brush products."

I drew in a long, cautious breath. The unmistakable fragrance of Here's My Heart perfume transported me back nearly twenty years.

"Why, this is my own handwriting!" I exclaimed as my eyes fell upon an invoice stapled to one of the bags. The untouched sack held more than a hundred dollars' worth of creams and colognes. This had been my very first sale to Mrs. Withers.

On that long-ago June day, I'd canvassed the wide, tree-lined avenue for nearly four hours, but not one lady of the house had invited me inside. As I rang the bell at the last house, I braced myself for the now-familiar rejection.

"Hello, ma'am, I'm your new Avon representative," I stammered, when the carved oak door swung open. "I have some great products I'd like to show you." When my eyes finally found the courage to face the lady in the doorway, I realized it was Mrs. Withers, the bubbly, matronly soprano in our church choir. I'd admired her lovely dresses and hats, dreaming that someday I'd wear

stylish clothes, too. Just two months
before, when I'd traveled to a distant city to have
brain surgery, Mrs. Withers had showered me with the
most beautiful cards.

"Why, Roberta, dear, come in, come in," Mrs.
Withers's voice sang out. "I need a million and one things.
I'm so glad you came to see me."

Gingerly, I eased myself onto the spotless white
sofa and unzipped my tweed satchel filled with all the cosmetic samples five dollars could buy. When I handed Mrs.
Withers a sales brochure, suddenly I felt like the most
important girl in the world.

Let us consider how we may spur one another
on toward love and good deeds.

HEBREWS 10:24, NIV

"Mrs. Withers, we have two types of creams, one for ruddy skin tones and another for sallow skin," I explained with newfound confidence. "And they're great for wrinkles, too."

"Oh good, good," she chirped.

"Which one would you like to try?" I asked, adjusting the wig hiding my stubbly surgery-scarred scalp.

"Oh, I'll surely need one of each," she answered. "And what do you have in the way of fragrances?"

"Here, try this one, Mrs. Withers. They recommend that you place it on the pulse point for the best effect," I instructed, pointing to her diamond-and-gold clad wrist.

"Why, Roberta, you're so knowledgeable about all of this. You must have studied for days. What an intelligent young woman you are!"

"You really think so, Mrs. Withers?"

"Oh, I know so. And just what do you plan to do with your earnings?"

"I'm saving for college to be a registered nurse," I replied, surprised at my own words. "But today, I'm thinking more of buying my mother a cardigan sweater for her birthday. She always goes with me for my medical treatments, and when we travel on the train, a sweater would be nice for her."

"Wonderful, Roberta, and so considerate. Now what do you have in the gift line?"

she asked, requesting two of each item I recommended.

Her extravagant order totaled $117.42. Had she meant to order so much? I wondered. But she smiled back and said, "I'll be looking forward to receiving my delivery, Roberta. Did you say next Tuesday?"

I was preparing to leave when Mrs. Withers said, "You look absolutely famished. Would you like some tea before you go? At our house, we think of tea as 'liquid sunshine.'"

I nodded, then followed Mrs. Withers to her pristine kitchen, filled with all manner of curiosities. I watched, spellbound, as she orchestrated a tea party like I'd seen in the movies just for me. She carefully filled the tea kettle with cold water, brought it to a "true" boil, then let the tea leaves steep for exactly five long minutes. "So the flavor will blossom," she explained.

Then she arranged a silver tray with a delicate

china tea set, a chintz tea cozy, tempting strawberry scones, and other small splendors. At home, we sometimes drank iced tea in jelly glasses, but never had I felt like a princess invited to afternoon tea.

"Excuse me, Mrs. Withers, but isn't there a faster way to fix tea?" I asked. "At home, we use tea bags."

Mrs. Withers wrapped her arm around my shoulder. "There are some things in life that shouldn't be hurried," she confided. "I've learned that brewing a proper pot of tea is a lot like living a proper life. It takes extra effort, but it's always worth it.

"Take you, for instance, with all of your health problems. Why, you're steeped with determination and ambition, just like a perfect pot of tea. Many people in your shoes would give up, but not you. You can accomplish anything you set your mind to, Roberta."

Abruptly, my journey back in time ended when

the lady in the hot, sticky attic asked, "You knew Hillary Withers, too?"

I wiped a stream of perspiration from my forehead. "Yes. I once sold her some of these cosmetics. But I can't understand why she never used them or gave them away."

"She did give a lot of them away," the lady replied matter-of-factly. "But somehow, some of them got missed and ended up here."

"But why did she buy them and not use them?" I asked.

"Oh, she purchased a special brand of cosmetics for her own use." The lady spoke in a confidential whisper. "Hillary had a soft spot in her heart for door-to-door sales-people. She never turned any of them away. She used to tell me, 'I could just give them money, but money alone doesn't buy self-respect. So I give them a little of my money, lend a listening ear, and share my love and prayers. You never know how far a little encouragement can take someone.'"

I paused, remembering how my cosmetic sales had soared after I'd first visited Mrs. Withers. I bought my mother the new sweater from my commission on the sale, and I still had enough money for my college fund. I even went on to win several district and national cosmetics-sales awards. Eventually, I put myself through college with my own earnings and realized my dream of becoming a registered nurse. Later, I earned a master's degree and a Ph.D.

"Mrs. Withers really cared for all of these people?" I asked, pointing to the dozens of timeworn delivery bags on the table.

"Oh, yes," she assured me. "She did it without the slightest desire that anyone would ever know."

I paid the cashier for my purchases—the sack of cosmetics I'd sold to Mrs. Withers, and a tiny, heart-shaped gold locket. I threaded the locket onto the gold chain I wore around my neck. Then I headed for the airport; later that afternoon I was addressing a medical convention in New York.

When I arrived in the elegant hotel ballroom, I found my way to the speaker's podium and scanned the sea of faces—health care specialists from all over the

country. Suddenly, I felt as insecure as on that long-ago day, peddling cosmetics in that unfamiliar, affluent neighborhood.

Can I do it? my mind questioned.

My trembling fingers reached upward to the locket. It opened, revealing a picture of Mrs. Withers inside. I again heard her soft but emphatic words: "You can accomplish anything you set your mind to, Roberta."

"Good afternoon," I began slowly. "Thank you for inviting me to speak about putting the care back in health

care. It's often said that nursing is love made visible. But this morning I learned an unexpected lesson about the power of quiet love expressed in secret. The kind of love expressed not for show, but for the good it can do in the lives of others. Some of our most important acts of love often go unnoticed. Until they've had some time to steep—for their flavor to blossom."

Then I told my colleagues the story of Hillary Withers. Much to my surprise, there was thunderous applause. And to think, it all began with a perfect pot of tea!

A Gift of Roses

AUTHOR UNKNOWN

An old man got on a bus one February 14 carrying a dozen red roses. He sat beside a young man. The young man looked at the roses and said, "Somebody's going to get a beautiful Valentine's Day gift."

"Yes," said the old man.

A few minutes went by and the old man noticed that his young companion was staring at the roses. "Do you have a girlfriend?" the old man asked.

"I do," said the young man. "I'm going to see her now. I'm taking her this." He held up a Valentine's Day card.

They rode along in silence for another ten minutes, and the old man rose to get off the bus. As he stepped out into the aisle, he suddenly placed the roses on the young man's lap and said, "I think my wife would want you to have these. I'll tell her that I gave them to you."

He left the bus quickly, and as the bus pulled away, the young man turned to see the old man enter the gates of a cemetery.

*To live in hearts we leave
Is not to die.*

THOMAS CAMPBELL

Sandcastles

MAX LUCADO

Hot sun. Salty air. Rhythmic waves. A little boy is on the beach. On his knees he scoops and packs the sand with plastic shovels into a bright red bucket. Then he upends the bucket on the surface and lifts it. And, to the delight of the little architect, a castle tower is created.

All afternoon he will work. Spooning out the moat. Packing the walls. Bottle tops will be sentries. Popsicle sticks will be bridges. A sandcastle will be built.

Big city. Busy streets. Rumbling traffic.

A man is in his office. At his desk he shuffles papers into stacks and delegates assignments. He cradles the phone on his shoulder and punches the keyboard with his fingers. Numbers are juggled and contracts are signed and, much to the delight of the man, a profit is made.

All his life he will work. Formulating the plans. Forecasting the future. Annuities will be sentries. Capital gains will be bridges. An empire will be built.

Two builders of two castles. They have much in common. They shape granules into grandeurs. They see nothing and make something. They are diligent and determined. And for both the tide will rise and the end will come.

Yet that is where the similarities cease. For the boy sees the end while the man ignores it. Watch the boy as the dusk approaches.

As the waves near, the wise child jumps to his feet and begins to clap. There is no sorrow. No fear. No regret. He knew this would happen. He is not surprised. And when the great breaker crashes into his castle and his masterpiece is sucked into the sea, he smiles. He smiles, picks up his tools, takes his father's hand, and goes home.

The grown-up, however, is not so wise. As the wave of years collapses on his castle he is terrified. He hovers over the sandy monument to protect it. He blocks the waves from the walls he has made. Saltwater soaked and shivering he snarls at the incoming tide.

"It's my castle," he defies.

The ocean need not respond. Both know to whom the sand belongs.

And I don't know much about sandcastles. But children do. Watch them and learn. Go ahead and build, but build with a child's heart. When the sun sets and the tides take—applaud. Salute the process of life, take your Father's hand, and go home.

Today is not yesterday—we ourselves change.
How then can our works and thoughts,
if they are always to be the fittest,
continue always the same.
Change, indeed, is painful, yet ever needful;
and if memory have its force and worth,
so also has hope.

THOMAS CARLYLE

Perspective

AUTHOR UNKNOWN

We do not understand:

Joy…until we face sorrow

Faith…until it is tested

Peace…until faced with conflict

Trust…until we are betrayed

Love…until it is lost

Hope…until confronted with doubts.

A Taste of Tea

RUTH BELL GRAHAM
from Legacy of a Pack Rat

In one of F. W. Boreham's books, he tells of an old Scottish woman living alone and very poor.

But she carefully tithed what little she had and gave to the church. When unable to attend service, she expected a deacon to drop by and collect her offering. The deacon knew well she could not afford it, but knowing also that she would be deeply offended if he did not collect it, he was careful to stop by.

It was late afternoon one day when he made his visit. Old Mary was sitting near a window having tea.

"The tithe is on the mantel," she said, greetings over. "Won't ye sit and have a cup of tea?"

The deacon sat, and when Mary passed him his

cup, he looked down in surprise and exclaimed:

"Why, Mary! It's only water ye have!"

"Aye!" said old Mary. "But He makes it taste like tea!"

It's a good thing to trust in providence. But I believe that the Almighty likes a little cooperation now and again.

FRANCES KEYES

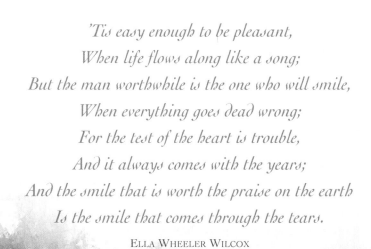

'Tis easy enough to be pleasant,
When life flows along like a song;
But the man worthwhile is the one who will smile,
When everything goes dead wrong;
For the test of the heart is trouble,
And it always comes with the years;
And the smile that is worth the praise on the earth
Is the smile that comes through the tears.

ELLA WHEELER WILCOX

*Try to make at least one person happy every day,
and then in ten years you may have made three
thousand, six hundred and fifty persons happy, or
brightened a small town by your contribution to the
fund of general enjoyment.*

SYDNEY SMITH

*Practice tenderhearted mercy and kindness to others.
Don't worry about making a good impression . . . be
gentle and ready to forgive; never hold grudges . . . most
of all, let love guide your life.*

COLOSSIANS 3:12–14, TLB

Gratuity

AUTHOR UNKNOWN

In all things showing yourself to be a pattern of good works...

TITUS 2:7, NKJV

In the days when an ice cream sundae cost much less, a ten-year-old boy entered a hotel coffee shop and sat at a table. A waitress put a glass of water in front of him.

"How much is an ice cream sundae?"

"Fifty cents," replied the waitress.

The little boy pulled his hand out of his pocket and studied a number of coins in it.

"How much is a dish of plain ice cream?" he inquired.

Some people were now waiting for a table and the waitress was a bit impatient.

"Thirty-five cents," she said brusquely.

The little boy again counted the coins. "I'll have the plain ice cream," he said.

The waitress brought the ice cream, put the bill on the table and walked away. The boy finished the ice cream, paid the cashier and departed. When the waitress came back, she began wiping down the table and then swallowed hard at what she saw. There, placed neatly beside the empty dish, were two nickels and five pennies—her tip.

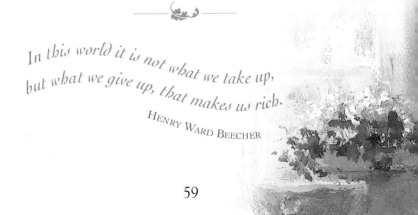

In this world it is not what we take up, but what we give up, that makes us rich.

HENRY WARD BEECHER

Shmily

LAURA JEANNE ALLEN

My grandparents were married for over half a century, and played their own special game from the time they had met each other. The goal of their game was to write the word "shmily" in a surprise place for the other to find. They took turns leaving "shmily" around the house, and as soon as one of them discovered it, it was their turn to hide it once more.

They dragged "shmily" with their fingers through the sugar and flour containers to await whoever was preparing the next meal. They smeared it in the dew on

the windows overlooking the patio where my grandma always fed us warm, homemade pudding with blue food coloring. "Shmily" was written in the steam left on the mirror after a hot shower, where it would reappear bath after bath. At one point, my grandmother even unrolled an entire roll of toilet paper to leave "shmily" on the very last sheet.

There was no end to the places "shmily" would pop up. Little notes with "shmily" scribbled hurriedly were

found on dashboards and car seats, or taped to steering wheels. The notes were stuffed inside shoes and left under pillows. "Shmily" was written in the dust upon the mantel and traced in the ashes of the fireplace. This mysterious word was as much a part of my grandparents' house as the furniture.

It took me a long time before I was able to fully appreciate my grandparents' game. Skepticism has kept me from believing in true love—one that is pure and enduring. However, I never doubted my grandparents' relationship. They had love down pat. It was more than their flirtatious little games; it was a way of life. Their relationship was based on a devotion and passionate affection which not everyone experiences.

Grandma and Grandpa held hands every chance they could. They stole kisses as they bumped into each other in their tiny kitchen. They finished each other's sentences and shared the daily crossword puzzle and word jumble. My grandma whispered to me about how cute my grandpa was, how handsome and old he had grown to be. She claimed that she really knew "how to pick 'em." Before every meal they bowed their heads and gave thanks, marveling at their blessings: a wonderful family, good fortune, and each other.

But there was a dark cloud in my grandparents' life—my grandmother had breast cancer. The disease had first appeared ten years earlier. As always, Grandpa was with her every step of the way. He comforted her in their yellow room, painted that way so that she could always be surrounded by sunshine, even when she was too sick to go outside.

Now the cancer was again attacking her body. With the help of a cane and my grandfather's steady hand, they went to church every Sunday. But my grandmother grew steadily weaker until, finally, she could not leave the house anymore. For a while, Grandpa would go to church alone, praying to God to watch over his wife. Then one day, what we all dreaded finally happened. Grandma was gone.

"Shmily." It was scrawled in yellow on the pink ribbons of my grandmother's funeral bouquet. As the crowd thinned and the last mourners turned to leave, my aunts, uncles, cousins and other family members came forward and gathered around Grandma one last time. Grandpa stepped up to my grandmother's casket and, taking a shaky breath, he began to sing to her. Through his tears and grief, the song came, a deep and throaty lullaby.

Shaking with my own sorrow, I will never forget

that moment. For I knew that, although I couldn't begin to fathom the depth of their love, I had been privileged to witness its unmatched beauty.

Shmily: See How Much I Love You.

I found him whom my soul loves.

SONG OF SOLOMON 3:4, NASB

Small Beginnings

HEATHER HARPHAM KOPP
from Patchwork of Love

Every friendship begins small.

Two smiles meet and

hold somehow.

But as each day passes,

Amid coffee or tea,

shared secrets and phone calls,

carpools and quilting bees—

a love grows large

enough to last into eternity.

Time and Tea

EMILIE BARNES
from If Teacups Could Talk

My granddaughter Christine and I are kindred spirits. We bonded when she was an infant—my first grandbaby. Our relationship has been special ever since, and tea parties have been part of that special relationship.

One Saturday afternoon as we were walking to the mailbox together, ten-year-old Christine said, "Grammy, let's make some scones and have tea."

The next thing I knew, we were in the kitchen whipping up our basic scone recipe. In just a matter of minutes we had popped them in the oven and were setting the table for a simple tea party—just Christine and me.

When the scones were done, we sat down. She poured the tea with practiced ease—we've done this before! We smeared the hot, tasty scones with our favorite jam and whipped topping.

But it's what happened next that made the afternoon so special. Once the tea was poured, we began to talk about friendships, parents, brothers (she has two), and what she could expect as a preadolescent. I was amazed at her knowledge and maturity. We ended up talking about spiritual matters—about God and the meaning of life.

It was only afterward, as I was carefully washing the china cups and returning them to their home in my oak armoire, that I realized what had happened that afternoon—Christine had asked for a tea party.

But what she was really asking for was time with me. Asking for tea was her way of saying "I need to talk to you."

Shepherd's Psalm

PSALM 23

The Lord is my shepherd; I shall not want.

He maketh me to lie down in green pastures;

he leadeth me beside the still waters.

He restoreth my soul; he leadeth me in the paths
of righteousness for his name's sake.

Yea, though I walk through the valley
of the shadow of death,
I will fear no evil; for thou art with me;
thy rod and thy staff they comfort me.

Thou preparest a table before me in the presence
of mine enemies; thou anointest my head with oil;
my cup runneth over.

Surely goodness and mercy shall follow me all the days of my life; and I will dwell in the house of the Lord forever.

Learned By Heart

TIM HANSEL
from You Gotta Keep Dancin'

The Lord is my shepherd, I shall not want.

PSALM 23:1, KJV

In his beautiful book, *I Shall Not Want*, Robert Ketchum tells of a Sunday school teacher who asked her group of children if anyone could quote the entire Twenty-third Psalm. A golden-haired four-and-a-half-year-old girl was among those who raised their hands. A bit skeptical, the teacher asked if she could really quote the entire psalm. The little girl came to the rostrum, faced the class, made a perky little bow, and said: "The Lord is my shepherd, that's all I want." She bowed again and went and sat down. That may well be the greatest interpretation I've ever heard.

Guard within yourself that treasure, kindness.
Know how to give without hesitation,
How to lose without regret,
How to acquire without meanness.
Know how to replace in your heart,
By the happiness of those you love,
The happiness that may be wanting
to yourself.

GEORGE SAND

Treasure

PAUL KORTEPETER

Years ago I found a solitary tea cup at an antique shop with a gorgeous pattern. I fell in love with it on the spot. From then on, I searched high and low for the rest of the set: in china shops, at auctions, flea markets, rummage sales…

Alas, without success. Not even a saucer!

Just as I was beginning to suspect that the cup wasn't part of a set at all, but a one-of-a-kind, never-to-be-found-again treasure, I was served tea on the very same china at the home of a friend.

Well, I stared with wide eyes until my friend said, "Isn't it beautiful? I found it at an estate sale. Unfortunately one of the cups is missing."

With a twinkle in my eye, I knew that my precious cup would soon have a new home.

Cheerfulness

HENRY WARD BEECHER

Cheerfulness . . . I cannot perhaps, exactly define what cheerfulness is, but you know what it is. You know the difference between a rusty piece of iron and a piece of iron that is polished. Take a piece of iron that is unpolished, and hold it up; it reflects nothing. Now polish it, and hold it up; how brilliant it looks! How every man and child delights to look at it! Now, the difference between polished iron and iron that is unpolished, is the difference between cheerfulness and no cheerfulness. Cheerfulness in a man is that which, when people meet him, makes them happy. A cheerful doctor gives his medicine the moment he steps inside the room . . . A clergyman, whose face glows with

health, and courage, and hope, and cheer, has looked con-
solation into his friend before he has spoken a word . . .
And in all the relations of life, the same is true. We find
that in the mind there is a provision for cheerfulness. And
cheerfulness gives pleasure.

Make me sufficient to my own occasions. Teach me to know and to observe the rules of the game. Give me to mind my own business at all times and to lose no good opportunity of holding my tongue. Let me never lack proper pride or a due sense of humor. Grant me neither to proffer nor to welcome cheap praise; to distinguish sharply between sentiment and sentimentality. Deliver me from emotional excess. Let me not dwell in the outer whirlwind of things and events; guide me . . . and grant that I may carry my cup brimming yet unspilled, to the last. Amen

ELIZA ATKINS STONE

Acknowledgments

A diligent search has been made to trace original ownership, and when necessary, permission to reprint has been obtained. If I have overlooked giving proper credit to anyone, please accept my apologies. Should any attribution be found to be incorrect, the publisher welcomes written documentation supporting correction for subsequent printings. For material not in the public domain, grateful acknowledgment is given to the publishers and individuals who have granted permission for use of their material.

Acknowledgments are listed by story title in the order they appear in the book. For permission to reprint any of the stories please request permission from the original source listed below.

"The Guest Book" by Carla Muir. © 1996. Used by permission of the author.

"That Little China Chip" by Bettie B. Youngs. Excerpted from VALUES FROM THE HEARTLAND, © 1995, Health Communications Inc. Used by permission.

"A Mailbox Mercy" by Nancy Jo Sullivan. Taken from MOMENTS OF GRACE by Nancy Jo Sullivan. © 2000. Used by permission of Multnomah Publishers, Inc.

"Picture of Peace" by Catherine Marshall. Taken from FRIENDS WITH GOD by Catherine Marshall, © 1956. Used by permission of Chosen Books, a division of Baker Book House Company.